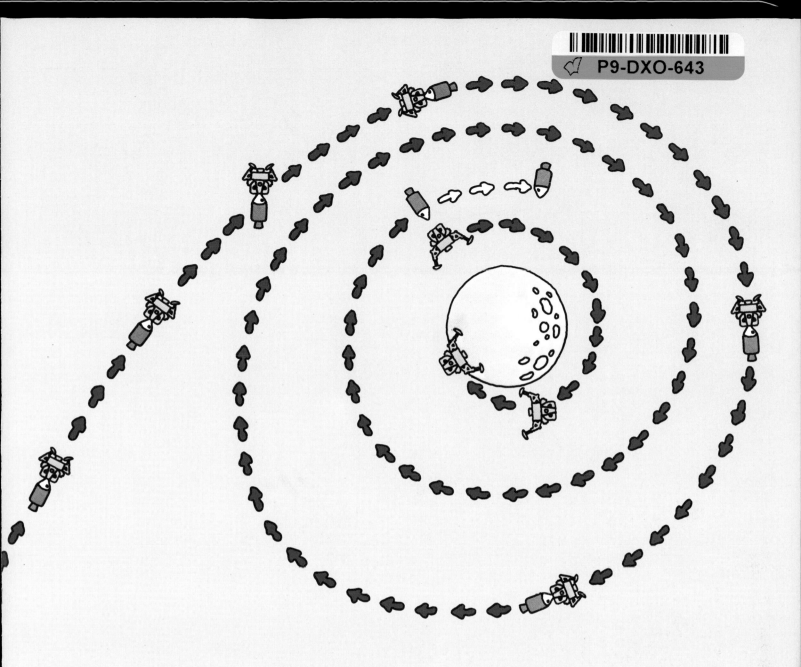

Going to the Moon

The red arrows show the path of the spaceship
from blast-off to landing. The three white arrows
show the path of the command module around the moon.

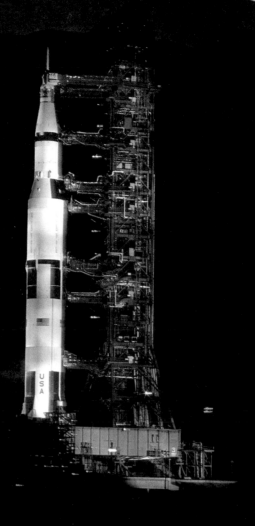

LET'S GO TO THE

moon

By Janis Knudsen Wheat

Drawings by Bill Burrows

☐ BOOKS FOR YOUNG EXPLORERS
NATIONAL GEOGRAPHIC SOCIETY

Copyright © 1977 National Geographic Society   Library of Congress CIP Data: page 32

Three astronauts are ready
to go to the moon.
They will travel in a spaceship.
The giant rocket will carry them
away from the earth,
far into space.
Each man wears
a space suit and helmet.
The astronauts go up the tower
and walk to the spaceship.
Soon they will begin
a great journey
to explore the moon.
Would you like to go along?

The spaceship
sits on top
of the mighty rocket.

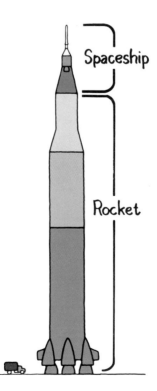

Spaceship

Rocket

3

Two workers wait
at the door
of the spaceship.
They shake hands
with each astronaut
and wish him
good luck.

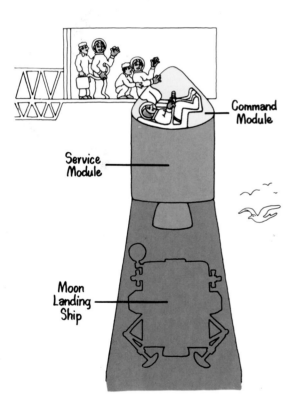

Command Module

Service Module

Moon Landing Ship

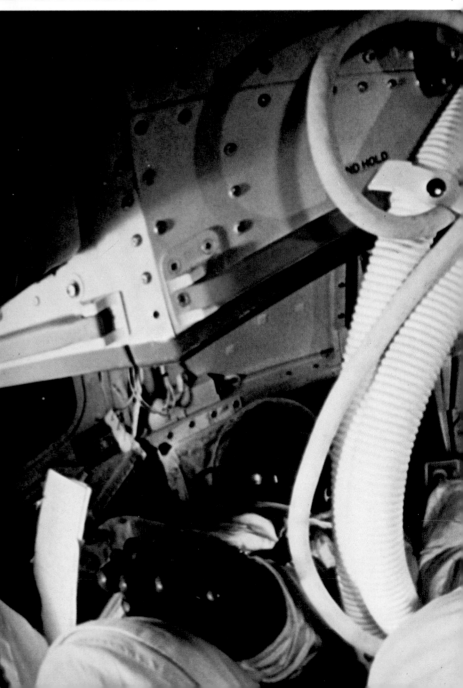

The astronauts climb through
a small door into the cabin
of the spaceship. This part
is called the command module.
The spaceship has
two other parts.
One is the service module.
The other part holds
the moon landing ship.

The men are strapped in their seats in the command module.
They will live and work here on their journey into space.
This small cabin will be their kitchen, bedroom, and office.
Just below them, the service module holds air and fuel
that the astronauts will need. Soon the rocket will be fired.
The countdown begins . . . 10 seconds, 9, 8, 7, 6.
One second to go and then . . .

Blast-off! White flames pour out of the rocket's engines.
With a great boom like thunder,
the rocket lifts up, up into the night sky.
Soon the fuel in the first part of the rocket burns up.
Then the engines in the second part of the rocket start.
The spaceship goes higher and higher, faster and faster.

The big rocket
is really three rockets
joined together.
When the first rocket
falls away
the second rocket
starts to burn.

Back on earth, scientists and workers watch
the astronauts and their spaceship night and day.
These scientists are at Mission Control in Texas.
They have equipment that tells them
if the spaceship is working just right.
Mission Control helps to keep the astronauts
on the right path to the moon.

In space, people and things float because they don't weigh anything at all.

It's breakfast time. An astronaut squirts juice into his mouth. Astronauts can't drink from a glass. Drops of juice would float around in the cabin. Do you see what happens when one man takes off his seat belt? He floats upside down. In space, fruit stays on a spoon, even when it is turned over.

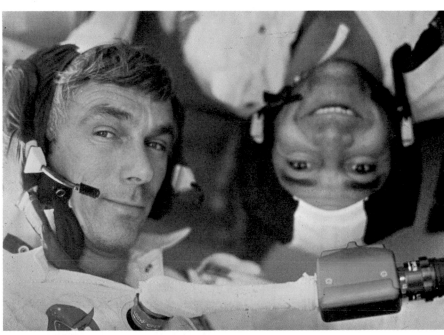

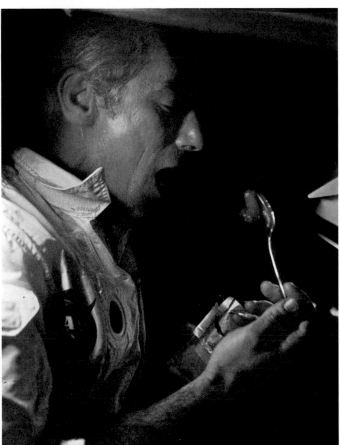

How strange it is to be in space!
The astronaut who took the first walk in space
was very brave, wasn't he? The long cord tied him
to the spaceship and kept him from floating away.
Other astronauts learned about living in space
from this first spacewalk.
All the astronauts trained for many years.
They practiced in a command module.
During training, the astronauts rode inside a plane.
When the plane was flown in a special way,
they floated inside the cabin.
This way they learned how it feels to be weightless.
Doesn't it look like fun!

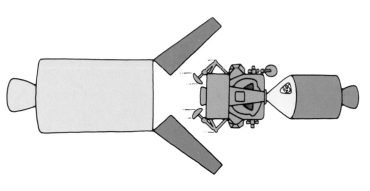

On their way, the astronauts turn
the command module around and pull
the moon landing ship out of the spaceship.

The trip to the moon takes three days.
Once the astronauts are on their way,
they do not wear their heavy space suits.
As the astronauts fly closer to the moon,
it looks larger and larger.
There are many holes, called craters, on the moon.

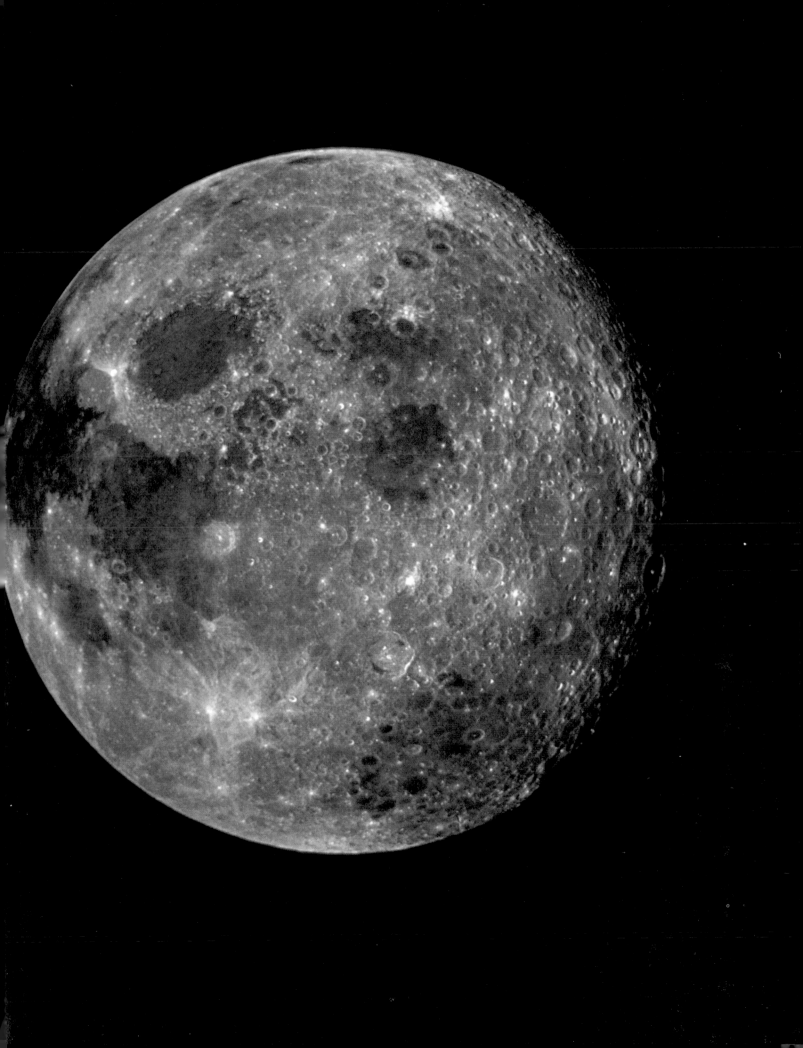

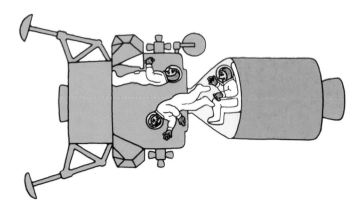

Two astronauts crawl
inside the moon landing ship.
The third man stays behind
in the command module.

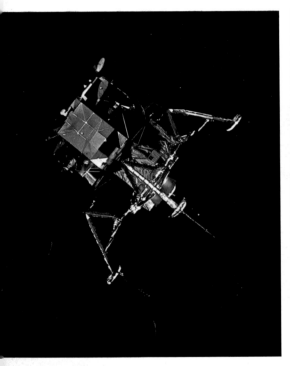

The men will land on the moon
in a landing ship called a lunar module or LEM.
It looks like a spider with long legs.
The LEM gets closer and closer. It lands with a little bump.
For the next six hours the astronauts get ready
to step out on the moon. They check their space suits
and equipment very carefully.
Finally an astronaut climbs down the ladder of the LEM.

ow the men
are on the moon!
This is a special moment,
and one of the astronauts
salutes the American flag.
All the people
who worked to send him
to the moon
feel very proud.
Beside the LEM
is a special moon car.
It is called the Rover
and was carried
to the moon in the LEM.
The astronauts will drive
it to explore the moon.
The moon does not look
like the earth at all.
There is no water, or air,
or grass. There is only
sand and rock.

As the astronauts explore the moon, they have many jobs to do. One astronaut drives the Rover. The other takes his picture. Then they go to collect rocks with a special rake. There is no air on the moon. But the space suits and backpacks hold air for the men to breathe. The pack also holds a radio, so the astronauts can talk to each other and to Mission Control on earth.

An astronaut finds a rock as big as a house.

Nothing lives or grows on the moon. Would you feel lonely there?

The lunar module
uses its rockets
to take off from the moon.
When it blasts off,
its landing legs
stay on the moon.

After three days, it is time to leave the moon. The LEM lifts off and flies up to the command module. In the distance, the astronauts see half of the earth in sunlight. It is night and dark on the other half. The astronaut in the command module has been flying around the moon. He has been waiting for the LEM and taking pictures. He is very happy when he sees the others again. Now all three men are together.

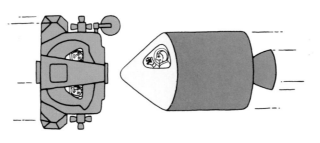

The astronauts join the LEM to the command module. Then the two men leave the LEM and crash it into the moon.

On the way home,
an astronaut opens the door
of the spaceship. He steps outside
into black, empty space.
Cameras outside the spaceship
took pictures of the moon.
The astronaut is bringing
the film back inside.
How beautiful the earth looks
from space! The oceans look blue.
The clouds and ice look white.
Soon the astronauts will be home.

Big parachutes open just before the spaceship lands
in the ocean. They help to slow the speed of the spaceship.
Splashdown! The spaceship hits the water with a great splash.
Balloons open to keep the spaceship from floating upside down.
Divers put a big orange float around it to keep
it from sinking. The divers help the astronauts into a raft.

A helicopter lifts the astronauts in a basket
and carries them to a ship waiting nearby.
Later the command module will be picked up too.
The safe and happy astronauts wave and smile
to everyone on the big ship.
Then, at last, they are with their families again.
Their fantastic journey into space is over.
But space adventures go on.
Maybe someday you too will take a trip into space.
You may even go to the moon.

Published by The National Geographic Society
Robert E. Doyle, *President;* Melvin M. Payne, *Chairman of the Board;*
Gilbert M. Grosvenor, *Editor;* Melville Bell Grosvenor, *Editor Emeritus*

Prepared by The Special Publications Division
Robert L. Breeden, *Editor*
Donald J. Crump, *Associate Editor*
Philip B. Silcott, *Senior Editor*
Cynthia Russ Ramsay, *Managing Editor*
Carolyn Leopold Michaels, *Researcher*
Jane G. Clarke, Wendy G. Rogers, *Communications Research Assistants*

Illustrations
Geraldine Linder, *Picture Editor*
Jody Bolt, *Art Director*
Suez B. Kehl, *Designer*
Lynda S. Petrini, *Design and Layout Assistant*

Production and Printing
Robert W. Messer, *Production Manager*
George V. White, *Assistant Production Manager*
Raja D. Murshed, June L. Graham, Christine A. Roberts, *Production Assistants*
Debra A. Antonini, Jane H. Buxton, Suzanne J. Jacobson, Cleo Petroff,
   Katheryn M. Slocum, Suzanne Venino, *Staff Assistants*

Consultants
Dr. Glenn O. Blough, Peter L. Munroe, *Educational Consultants*
Edith K. Chasnov, *Reading Consultant*
Dr. Farouk El-Baz, Walter J. Dillon, Air and Space Museum, Smithsonian Institution; Les Gaver, William J. O'Donnell, NASA; the crew of Apollo 17: Capt. Eugene A. Cernan, USN, Ret., Capt. Ronald E. Evans, USN, Ret., and Senator Harrison H. Schmitt, *Scientific Consultants*.

Illustrations Credits
NASA: Apollo 17 (2 top left and right, 4 top, 6-7, 15, 26 bottom, 27, 28, 29, 30, 31 left); Apollo 11 (2 bottom, 7 bottom); Apollo 8 (4-5); Apollo 5 (8 top); Apollo 14 (8-9); Harrison H. Schmitt, Apollo 17 (10-11, 11 top, 20 top); Ronald E. Evans, Apollo 17 (11 bottom, 14 top); James A. McDivitt, Gemini 4 (12-13); Eugene A. Cernan, Apollo 17 (14 bottom, 20-21, 21 top, 22-23, 25 top); Michael Collins, Apollo 11 (16 left, 24-25); Richard F. Gordon, Jr., Apollo 12 (16 right); Neil A. Armstrong, Apollo 11 (17, 32); David R. Scott, Apollo 15 (18-19); Apollo 16 (21 bottom); Skylab (25 bottom); Russell L. Schweickart, Apollo 9 (26 top). David Moore and Michael S. Bolden, National Geographic Staff (1); Sallie M. Greenwood, National Geographic Staff (3 left); Albert Moldvay (12 top); Ralph Morse, Life (12 bottom); Jon Schneeberger, National Geographic Staff (31 right).

Cover Photograph: NASA, Eugene A. Cernan, Apollo 17   Endsheet: Bill Burrows
Library of Congress CIP Data
Wheat, Janis Knudsen, 1937-   Let's go to the moon.   (Books for young explorers)
SUMMARY: Highlights the journey of Apollo 17 through space to the moon and back to earth.
1. Project Apollo—Juvenile literature. 2. Space flight to the moon—Juvenile literature. [1. Project Apollo. 2. Space flight to the moon] I. Burrows, Bill. II. Title. III. Series.
TL789.U6A665   629.43'53   77-76972   ISBN 0-87044-244-9

This footprint on the moon
will stay for thousands of years.
There is no wind or rain
to wear it away.

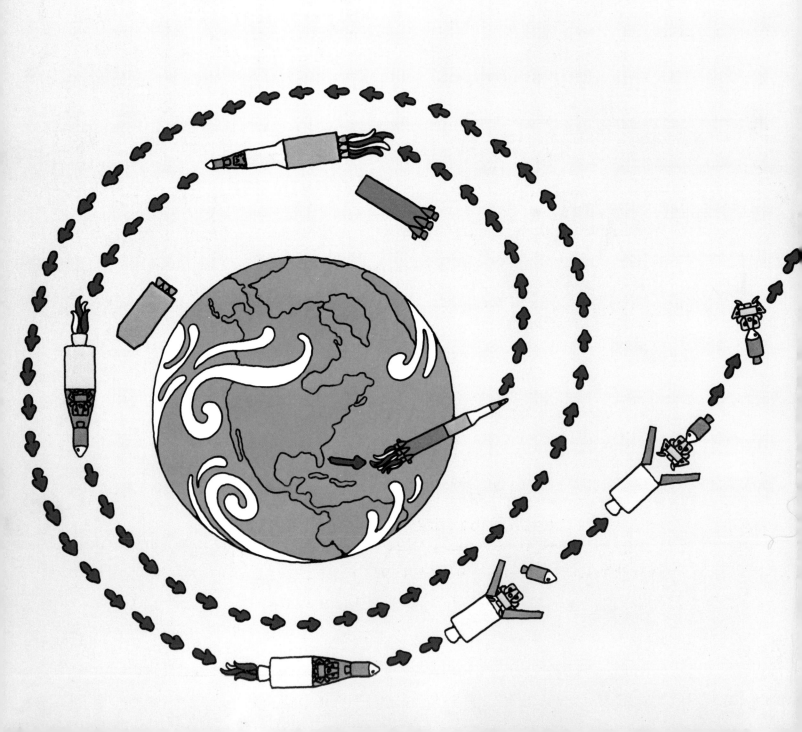